Written and compiled by Pedro Cuencas-Michel
Illustrated by David Sells

For all the fellow riddle lovers out there

**We would like to thank the following people for
all of their help, encouragement, and inspiration**

Ramon & Trini Cuencas, Robbie & Deborah Sells,
Marisol Cuencas, Anna Sells, James Sells, Wendy Pereira,
Oscar F. Michel, Gerald Coddington, Jamie Williams,
Jimmie Weinman, Brian & Kerri Moore, Steven Lorio,
Renee Stevenson, Jeremy & Christin Herron, Helen Wood,
Brad Boss, The Roy Ross Family, Melissa Flandreau,
Robert Kiyosaki, Robert Allen, Napolean Hill
and John Rieck.

A little riddle background

Riddle, a deliberately enigmatic or ambiguous question requiring a thoughtful and often witty answer.

A riddle is a form of guessing game that has been part of the folklore from ancient times in most cutures. Western scholars generally recognize two main kinds of riddle: the descriptive riddle and the shrewd or witty question.

In this book, you will find both descriptive and witty riddles in both poem form and question form.

The people who answer correctly are not necessarily the smartest, but rather, they use their imagination to see the riddle differently.

So whether you get it right or not, a riddle will make you see things differently and help develop your imagination. Riddles are an entertaining way to stimulate the mind and force those brain cells to be more creative.

Not quite a kiss,

But more than a shake.

Easy to give,

But takes two to make.

Tight or light;

It will all depend,

On the love you want

To share and extend.

Twisted ladders you cannot climb.
We are passed along over time.
And though this sounds a bit bizarre,
We will define who you are.

What are we?

We are a family of rectangles decorated with dots.

Each member is special,
Each with their own spots.

You can place them together whenever you play.

But make sure they are facing the proper way.

What are the rectangles?

I dig out tiny caves and store
gold and silver in them.

I also build build bridges of silver
and make crowns of gold.

Sooner or later everybody needs
my help, yet many people are afraid
to let me help them.

Who am I?

You throw away the outside and cook the inside.

Then, you eat the outside and throw away the inside.

What vegetable did you eat?

Old and dated it cannot be.

Fresh and current is the key.

Through the air, paper, and TV;

It is delivered on all three.

What is it?

Before a test, you better take.

The music always ought to make.

Pass around between two at least.

A gossip lover's silent feast.

What is being described?

A place where the water comes to greet.

It kisses your feet, then leaves in retreat.

A place where it seems heavy to walk and harder to run, yet everyone comes to have some fun.

What is this place?

A time when they're green.
A time when they're brown.
But both of these times,
Cause me to frown.

But just in between,
For a very short while,
They're perfect and yellow,
And cause me to smile!

What am I talking about here?

The maker doesn't want it,
the buyer doesn't use it,
and the user doesn't see it.

What is it?

A man pushed his car. He stopped when he reached a hotel, at which point he knew he was bankrupt.

Why?

I admit, I am a tree.
But let me ask you this first.

What kind of tree is found
on your hand, and can also
quench your thirst?

It is quieter than silence, and bigger than infinity.

Dead people eat this - and if and if you eat it, you die too.

What is it?

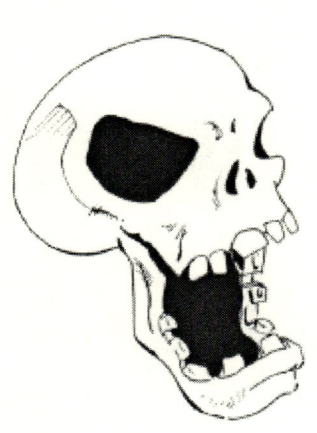

What is the only place in town where you can see the imagination of thousands of people, learn about anything without listening to a teacher, and take home the great minds of our time, and do this all for free?

When you say my name,
I no longer exist.

What am I?

Seems like everywhere you go,
there we are; rolling below.
But if one of us cannot roll on,
you have to stop and show your brawn.
It will happen when you least expect,
but less often if you keep us checked.

What are we?

Black when you buy it,
Red while you use it,
White when you are done.

What is it?

Add up the bill,
Or leave it to me.
You can crunch the cereal,
Leave the numbers to me.
You will get the right answer,
All straight in a row.
Just push the right buttons,
On my body below.

What am I?

In what sport do the winners go backward, and the losers go forward?

I am a weapon of choice for a friendly fight.

But I will keep you in comfort throughout the night.

All alone I become a little more puffed.

Even though I don't eat, boy am I stuffed!

What am I?

Always old, sometimes new.

Never sad, sometimes blue.

Never empty, sometimes full.

What am I?

Are we good or bad?
One positive side, and one negative side.
Equally balanced, so it's hard to decide.

We will give you the power,
So you be the judge.
When you put us in place,
With a slide and a nudge.

What are we?

In the cellar there are three light switches in the OFF position. Each switch controls one of the three lights on the floor above. You may only go upstairs once to inspect the bulbs.

How can you determine which switch controls which bulb with only one trip upstairs?

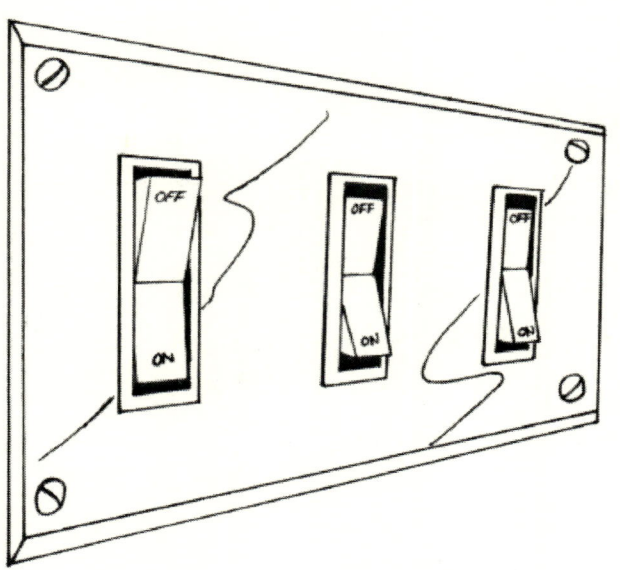

If you find me on the road,
Do not panic - it's okay.
I belong on the farm pitching the hay.
But you can always find me at any buffet.

What am I?

When I am needed,
They throw me out.
When I am not needed,
They bring me in.

What am I?

Look straight through me.
You might find a clue.
Round with a handle.
I can start fires too.

What am I ?

Runs but has no legs,

Has a mouth but does not speak,

Has a bed but does not sleep.

What is it?

I start off liquid,
but end up solid.
Add a little butter,
and some syrup too.
A well rounded meal,
Made from goo.

What am I?

An Arab man tells his two sons to race their camels to a distant city to see who will inherit his fortune. He says, "The one whose camel is slowest will win."

Confused, the brothers wonder aimlessly for days, until finally they ask a wise man for advice. After hearing the advice, they jump on the camels and race as fast as they can to the city.

What does the wise man say?

I have claws and a tail,
but I am not a cat.
I am long and red,
but I am not a fox.
Believe me when I tell you,
I am quite a catch.
A fancy dinner,
with a price to match.

What am I?

A man was driving along the highway in his old car, when suddenly the car shifted gears by itself. However, the man was not concerned and kept on driving.

Why wasn't he concerned?

All day long we hang around,
Waiting for you to change around.

Push us left and push us right.

Only you can decide how you look tonight.

What are we?

A snail is at the bottom of a well 30 feet deep. It crawls up 3 feet each day, but at night, it slips down 2 feet.

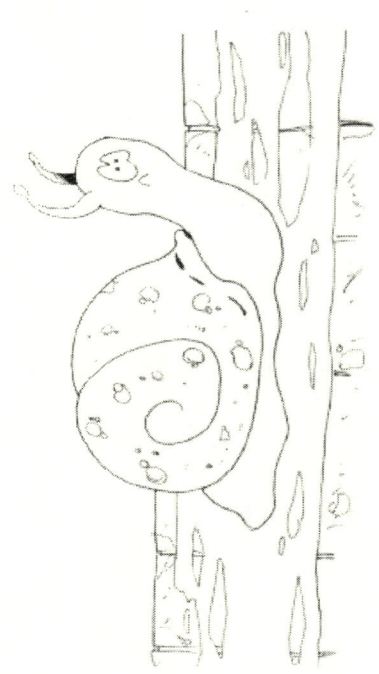

How long does it take for the snail to crawl out of the well?

A little yellow man,
Built rough and tough.
But put him in a heated pan
and discover he's all fluff.

What is it?

In the year 1990, a person is 15 years old. In 1995, that same person is 10 years old.

How is that possible?

There is a place where you can find plenty of things for sale. The problem, you don't know how much anything costs when you get there. In fact, if you don't go, something might be sold cheaper than if you had decided to go.

What is this place?

Before Mount Everest was discovered, what was the highest mountain on earth?

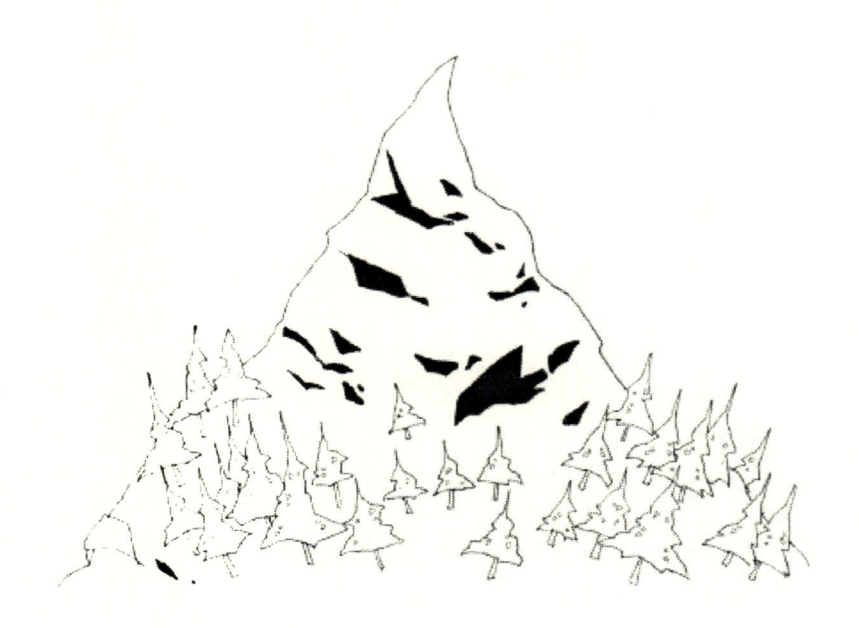

John was very impressed when he saw the masterpiece in front of him.
"Perfect," he said as he fiddled with the keys. Finally, he could play his music loud. He took a seat and noticed it had nice pedals. It had just been in for a tune-up. But, if there was a problem with it, they could fix it by lifting the top.

John wasn't admiring any kind of automobile. What was he looking at?

I cannot be felt, seen, or touched,
Yet, I can be found in everybody.
My existence is always in debate,
Yet, I have my own style of music.

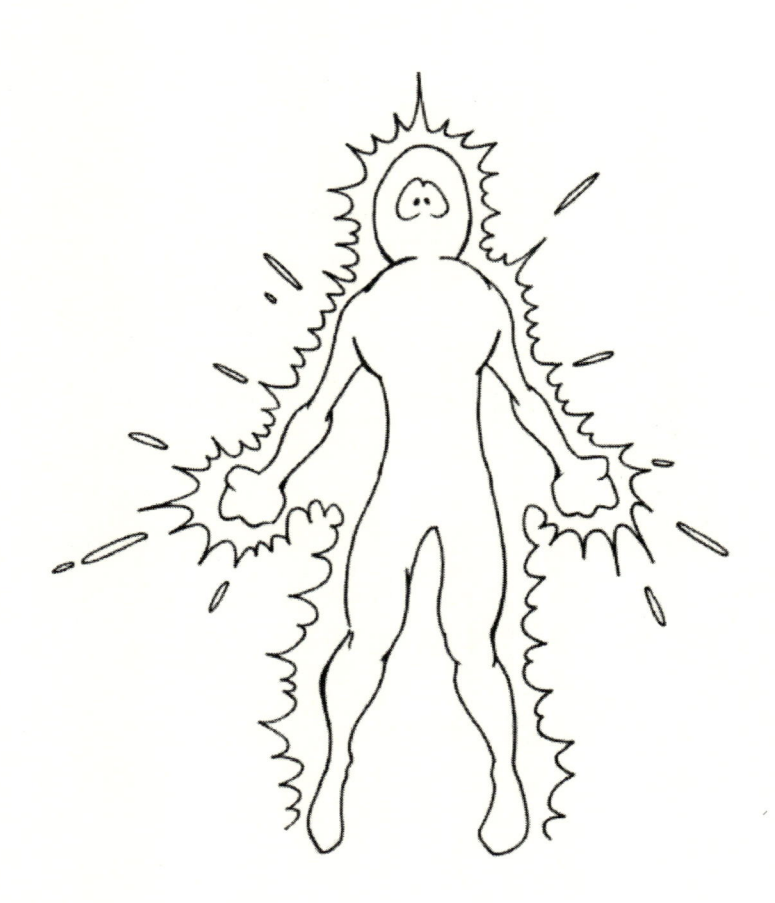

What am I ?

Two rows of teeth come together as one,

A breeze you will feel if we come undone.

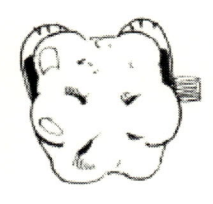

What is being described?

If you were running a race, and you passed the person in 2nd place, what place would you be in?

What is cheaper?

Taking one friend to the movies twice.

OR

Taking two friends to the movies once.

They call me a man,
but I'll never have a wife.
I was given a body,
but not given life.
They made me a mouth,
but didn't give me breath.
Water gives me life,
and sun brings me death.

What am I?

You have two clocks.

One is stopped (it doesn't work), and the other is one minute slow.

Which clock is more exact?

A plane crashed and every single person on board was killed.

Yet, there were survivors.

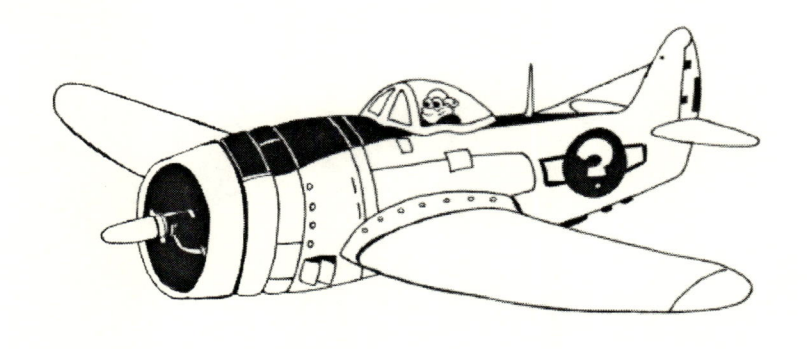

Explain how.

A train takes off from New York to Los Angeles. Another train takes off from Los Angeles to New York going twice as fast. When the trains cross paths, which train is closer to New York?

What can be driven,
but has no wheels.
And can be sliced,
but still remain whole?

What kind of book can an author never finish completely?

Which moves faster: heat or cold?
(Humorous answer)

A long time ago there were kings that built magnificent structures which they filled with treasure and their most precious things. However, the kings never lived there. In fact, no one lived there. These structures are still around today.

What are they?

A doctor and a bus driver are both in love with the same woman, a sweet girl named Wendy. The bus driver had to go on a long bus trip that would last a week. Before he left, he gave Wendy seven apples.

Why??

They come to me in masses
for the masses or some classes.
As baskets make their passes, a
special hour passes.

What am I?

You do not want to have it.
But when you do have it,
You do not want to lose it.

What is it?

A leader in the shaving business,
I was born to make a point, Helping
people write and draw,
I never disappoint.

What am I?

If you were to spell out numbers, how far would you have to go until you found the letter "A"?

I can burn you and sting you,
but I don't like to boast.

You might find me floating right next
to the coast.

You can see through my body,
but I was never a ghost.

Basically, I am jelly, but don't put me
on toast.

What am I ?

What is the least number of chairs you would need around a table to sit 4 fathers, 2 sons, and two grandfathers?

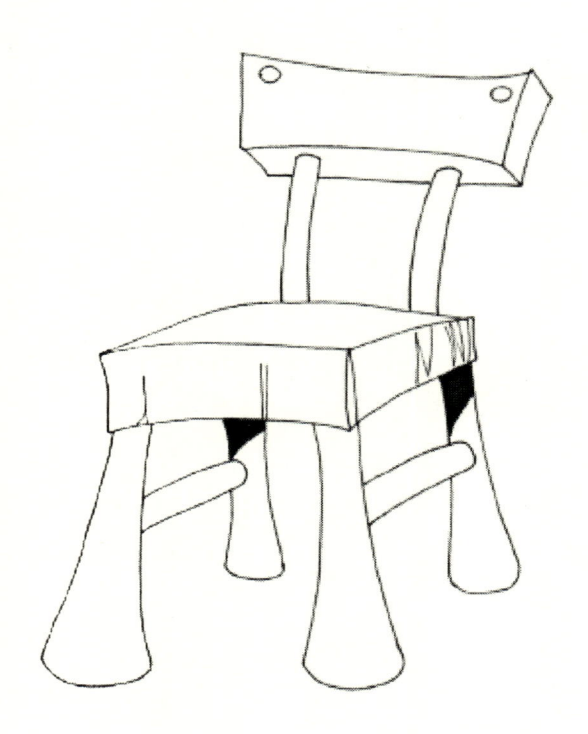

There is one in every well-kept home,
Loud and flat the plains they roam,
It is a proven fact that they all suck,
They do their job when the switch is struck.

What are they?

The beginning of eternity,
The end of time and space,
The beginning of every end,
And the end of every place.

What am I?

To conquer me you must last twenty-six.
You may run, walk, or do a mix.

To excel you must train or face defeat.
But to simply finish is a worthy feat.

What is being described?

I have 10 red socks and 10 blue socks in a drawer.

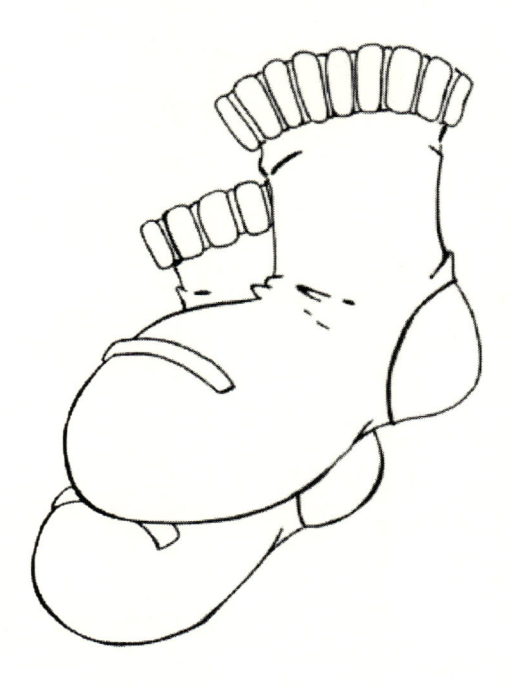

How many socks must I take out to ensure that I have at least one matching pair?

How many do I have to pull out to ensure that I have at least one pair of red and one pair of blue?

What lies down when you stand up and stands up when you lie down?

A murderer is condemned to death. He has to choose between three rooms.

The first is full of raging fires, the second is full of assassins with loaded guns, and the third is full of lions that haven't eaten in 3 years.

Which room is safest for him?

Like a snake with two buck teeth,
I curl out from beneath.

Though have no fear, I do no harm.
When my fangs go in, do not be alarmed.

I will help you sometime today,
To light your lamp or hear music play.

What am I?

If you take off my skin, I will not cry, but you will!

What am I?

The early Romans used it for identification.

In other cultures it marks a special occasion.

Nowadays, it's still a painful decoration.

What is it?

What is the maximum amount of money you can have in coins and still not be able to make exact change for a dollar?

(using quarters, dimes, nickels, and pennies)

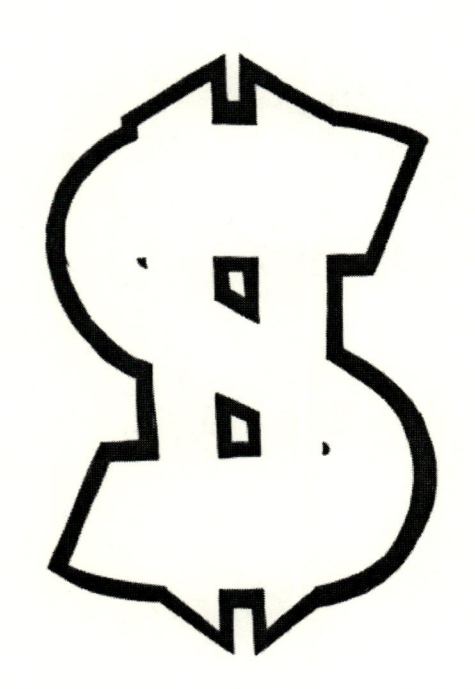

Call my number but hear no voice,
Instead you hear a long strange noise,
Luckily, that's a perfect sign,
To send your stuff through my line.

What am I?

There is a green house.

Inside the green house is a white house.

Inside the white house is a red house.

Inside the red house are babies that will grow to be green houses.

What is the green house?

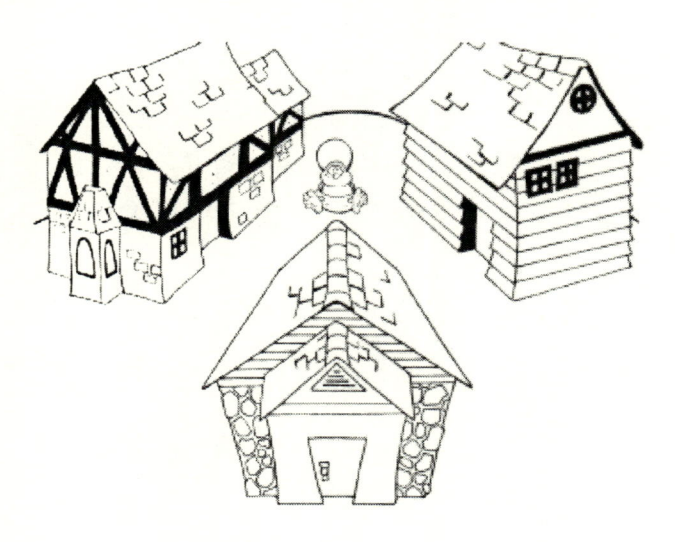

We are on some clothes, and on some faces.
Usually unwelcome in both places.

So try some cream, or try dry clean, and pray we vanish like a dream.

What are we?

There is a certain crime.

If attempted, it is punishable, but if committed, it is not punishable.

What is the crime?

The strangest creature you'll ever find.

Has two eyes in front and a hundred behind.

What animal is being described?

When can you add two to eleven and get one as the correct answer?

11 + 2 = 1

Millions of men wake up every morning and start off the day by tightening a noose around their neck.

What are these men doing?

Brad Doe works for a packaging company. One day, he received four separate orders and accidentally mixed up the addresses, so he applied the addresses at random.

What is the probability that exactly three packages were correctly labeled?

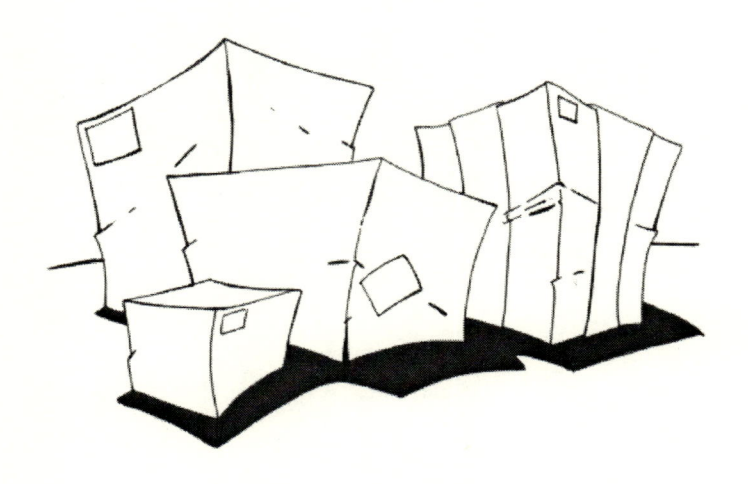

From the cane or from the beet.
Either way made very sweet.
The plants I help, and please
observe; I am energy put on
reserve.

What am I?

There is an invention still used in most parts of the world today that allows people to see through walls.

What is it?

If your day is looking not so bright, I should tag along; need me you might.

When the time comes, open and spread. Protecting you from overhead.

What am I?

He has married many women,
but has never been married.

Who is he?

For a child it is hard to go through.
What was once united, is now two.
First I do, then we do not.
A broken home; untie the knot.

What is it?

The pope has it,
but he does not use it.

Your father has it and your
mother uses it.

Nuns do not need it.

What is it?

There is an object that shoots people, but instead of killing them, it preserves their image for future generations.

What is it?

Six glasses are in a row. The first three are filled with milk, and the last three are empty.

By moving only one glass, can you arrange them so that the full and the empty glasses alternate?

Tall giants with one big bright eye.
They may spot you floating by.
To their duty they stand proud and true,
At night they light the rocky blue.

What are the giants?

Here on Earth it's always true that tomorrow will follow today. Yet there is a place where yesterday always follows today.

Where is this place?

What do people pay for every month, hoping they don't have to use it?

What is it that you must give before you can keep it?

Sprinkled with color,
Or simply glazed over.
A hole in the middle.
Can you solve this riddle?

I demand you to answer,
but I ask no question.

What am I?

What becomes visible only when you raise your arm?

He who breaks me is proud.
And once broken, I am harder
to break again.

What am I?

Rock and stone on royal land,
But more often made from sand.

In the past was made to last,
On the beach, crush with your feet.

What is it?

What kind of ship has two mates but no captain?

A small explosion that must be expressed.

But afterwards, you should be blessed.

What is it?

Some months have thirty days and some months have thirty-one days.

How many months have twenty-eight days?

We are leaders full of energy.
All smiles, and good agility.
When the game is great,
or just plain lame,
Look our way, we entertain.

What are we?

What starts with T, ends with T, and is full of T?

All of my flowers except
two are roses.

All of my flowers except
two are tuplips.

All of my flowers except
two are daisies.

How many flowers do I have?

What is it that everyone needs, everyone gives, everyone asks for, and that very few take?

We travel in armies,
Armed with a bite.

Stay away from our hill,
We will put up a fight.

Do not underestimate the size
of our hate.

Watch as we carry twenty times
our own weight.

What are we?

Four jolly men sat down to play,
and played all day till the break of day.
They played for cash and not for fun,
With a separate score for every one.
When it came to square accounts,
They all had made quite fair amounts.
Not one had lost and all had gained.
Tell me now, this can you explain?

What were the men doing?

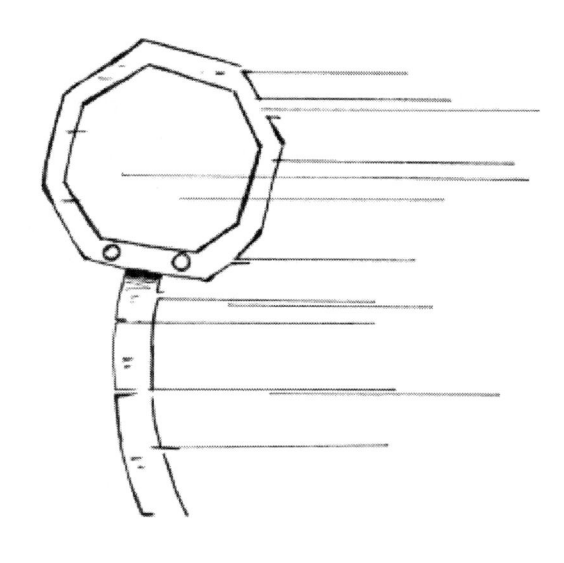

A brief little signal,
It happens so quick.
Just open and close,
There is truly no trick.
As soon as you see it,
You may stop and think;
Was that a flirt,
Or half of a blink?

What gets harder to catch the faster you run?

I am normally asleep,
and be thankful I am.

If I ever wake up, you
better scram.

Darkness I bring to my
neighboring turf.

From my mouth comes hot,
heated earth.

The more you take,
the more you leave behind.

What are they?

I have a first name,
but a last name I lack.

Watch were I am going;
Make sure you keep track.

Be not fooled by the calm in my eye;

For soon from above, I will strike from the sky.

What am I?

Take away the whole,
and you still have some left.

Take away some,
and you still have the whole left.

What is it?

For long trips I pack my trunk.
For short trips I take it too.
In fact, I take it everywhere.
Come see me at the zoo.

What am I?

The more I dry,
the wetter I become.

What am I?

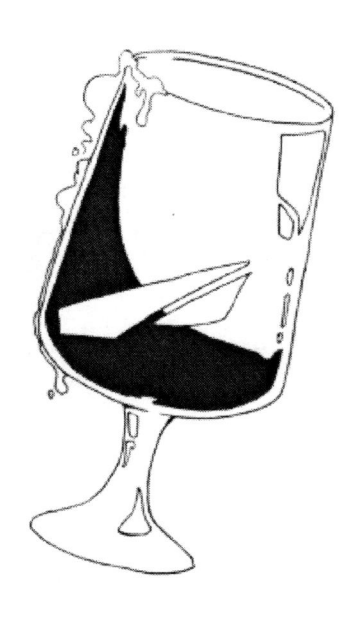

I am made when the glass is raised,
To celebrate, rejoice, or praise.
Do not be shy and please stand up.
Be loud, be bold, and lift yours up.

What is being described?

If you have it, you want to share it.
But if you share it, you don't have it.

What is it?

They will save your life on
a summer day,

But wait too long and they will
go away.

Drop them in; they do not sink.

Just be concerned with how you
like your drink.

What are they?

What are the four words you can make out of the letters N, E, M, A, using all the letters?

People hit me when they want to play.
They strike my head and pound away.
Now I must confess it is pretty neat.
At times they seem to make a beat.

What am I?

If you do it regularly,
you are considered a good citizen.

If you do it twice on the same day,
it's a serious crime.

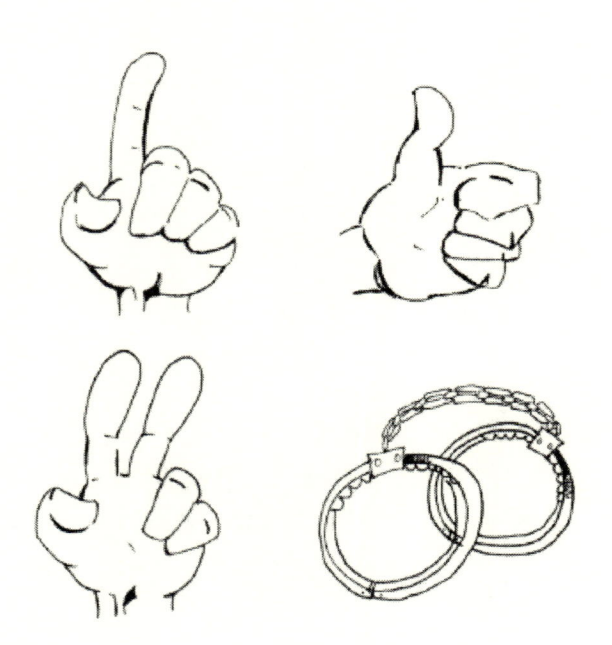

What is it?

Who...Who....
Who turned on the lights?
I do not mind, but I prefer the nights.
That is when I go to hunt.
I can turn my neck from back to front.

What am I ?

What do you have sitting down that you don't have standing up?

Something that makes your stomach shake.
It might even make your tummy ache.
But doctors say it is good for you.
So go ahead and make it work for you!

What is it?

I went into the woods and got it.
I sat down to seek it.
I brought it home with me,
because I couldn't find it.

What is it?

I sprout from the ground,
But I was never a seed.
Can you eat me? - Yes indeed.
I wear a cap, and you can eat that too.
As a caution, I should warn you.
Beware of my bothers.
They will poison you.

What am I?

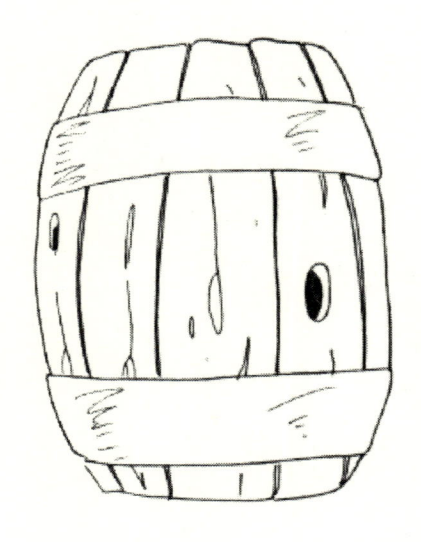

What can you put in a barrel to make it weigh less?

We were created one hundred miles
beneath the earth, so that should justify
our costly worth.

While people dig to find us deep and
dark, you can find us at a baseball park.

And if you cannot leave your house,
there is hope, so have no shame.
Invite your friends, and for those who
came, you can find us in a poker game.

What are we?

When young,
I am sweet in the sun.

When middle-aged,
I can make you mellow.

When old,
I am valued more than ever.

What am I?

I am an engine that can take you to any address you wish to go.

To start the engine, you will need more than one key. In fact, you will need several keys below.

No matter the destination, you will arrive without ever leaving your chair.

Search the spider's home, and find my domain there.

What is being described?

My life can be measured in hours.
I serve by being devoured.

Thin, I am quick;
Fat, I am slow.
Wind is my foe.

What am I ?

In the distance I heard a pleasant tune,
A common sound through the month of June.
As it neared, it warmed my heart.
The sound meant coldness, ice, my favorite part.
I could not resist the tempting freeze.
I approached and paid, and watched it leave.
The tune was gone, but I must say,
I beat the heat, and was very pleased.

What was the tune?

I run over fields and woods all day.
Under the bed at night I sit not alone.
My tongue hangs out, up and to the rear, awaiting to be filled in the morning.

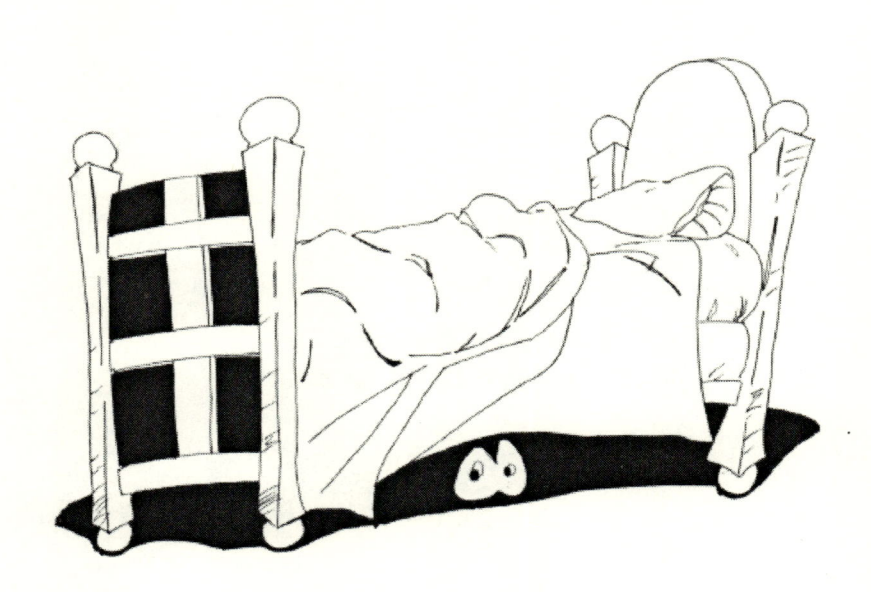

What am I?

On women we may be long.
On men we are typically short.
Keep us clean,
And keep us white,
Or we get black;
A dirty sight.

What are we?

The more there is,
the less you see.

What is it?

A stout, red, muscle man who is responsible for your life.

He never stops,
He never sleeps,
The rhythm of life,
He makes the beats.

Who is he?

Take one out and scratch my head.
I am now black, but once was red.

I am your equal in skill
and also in stature.

I am used in heat and light
manufacture.

What am I?

131

When you approach me, do not be shy.
I may flash my rounded bright green
eyes.

Respect my moods; I am the law.
I confess my timing may have some
flaws.

Be alert, for when I blink, your foot may
have to switch and sink.

What am I?

It takes Alicia 3 hours to paint a fence, and it takes Mark 6 hours to complete the same job.

How long would it take both of them working together at their normal pace to complete the same job?

A monster at sea that reveals only his head.

It has crushed many a ship, and left many more dead.

So be careful as you sail through the omnious mist.

It attacks with a powerful, ice-cold kiss.

What is it?

A butcher is 5 feet 10 inches tall.

What does he weigh?

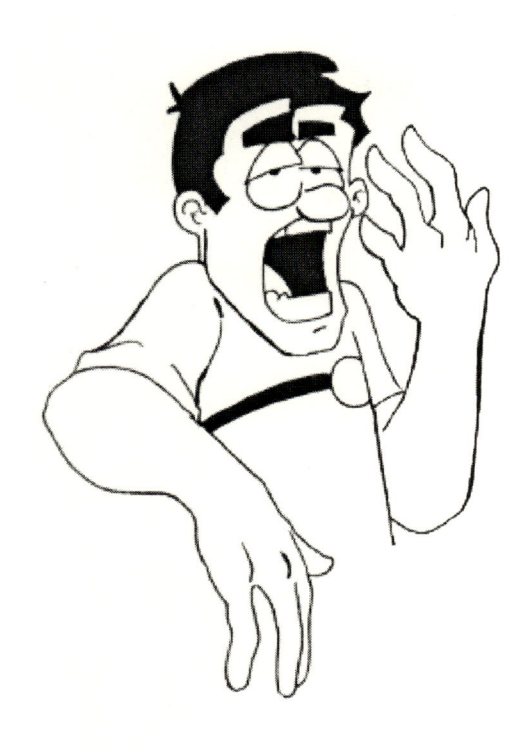

If you take me you will fall asleep.
But I am not something you can
eat or drink.

Not liquid, solid, gas, or mass.
I am not allowed during any class.

What am I?

Never resting, never still;
Moving silently from hill to hill.
It does not walk, run, or trot.
All is cool where it is not.

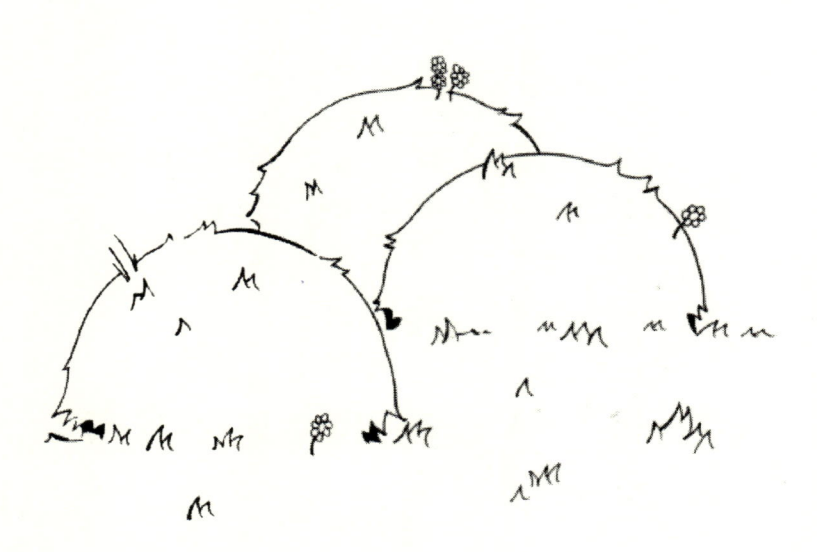

What is it?

A crayon for women that is used with a twist.

Only two lines are drawn,
Every other place missed.

What is the crayon?

Mr. and Mrs. Smith were walking home from the shopping mall with their purchases when Mr. Smith began to complain that his load was too heavy.

Mrs. Smith turned to her husband and said, "I don't know what you are complaining about because if you gave me one of your parcels, I would have twice as many as you. And if I gave you just one of mine, we would have equal loads."

How many parcels were each carrying?

What sea creature is a thousand times more valuable when it is injured than when it is perfectly healthy?

Mr and Mrs. Mustard have six daughters and each daughter has one brother. How many people are in the Mustard family?

You can find roads without cars,
Forests without trees,
Cities without houses.
Whatever can I be?

Late afternoons I often bathe.
I'll soak in water piping hot.
My essence goes through my
see-through clothes.
Used up am I; I've gone to pot.

What am I?

Pronounced as one letter,
But look and you'll see,
That I'm really written with three.
I am read from both ends,
The same either way.

What am I?

I come in darkness,
but fill the mind with light.

I bring enlightenment to some,
while gripping others with fear.

What I will show you will often
be unreachable.

Journey with me and what you
see may haunt you.

Journey with me and you may
never want to return home.

Journey with me and you will
never know when it will end.

What am I?

Man walks over,
Man walks under,
In times of war,
He burns asunder.

What is it?

It is part of us,
and then replaced.

It escapes our bodies
to a better place.

The world becomes
its sizable home;
Bringing to life the
planet it roams.

What is it?

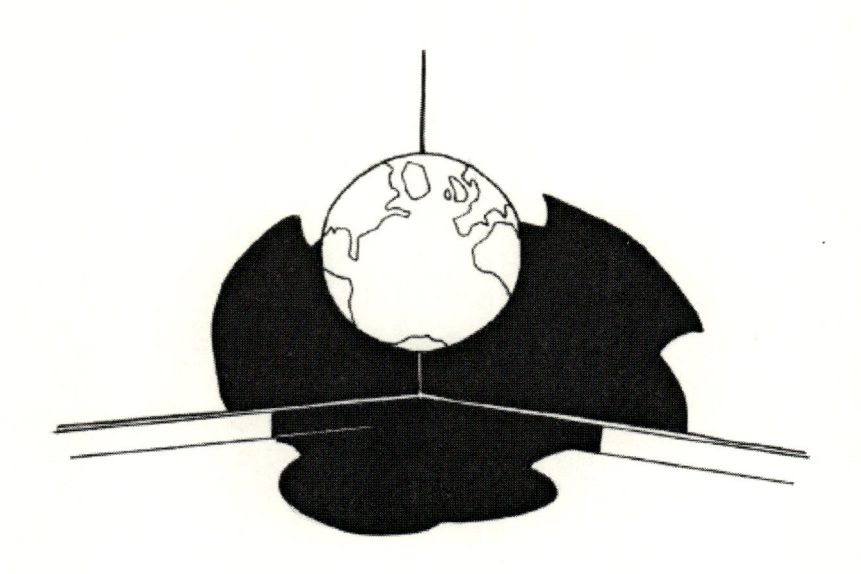

What word becomes shorter when you add two letters to it?

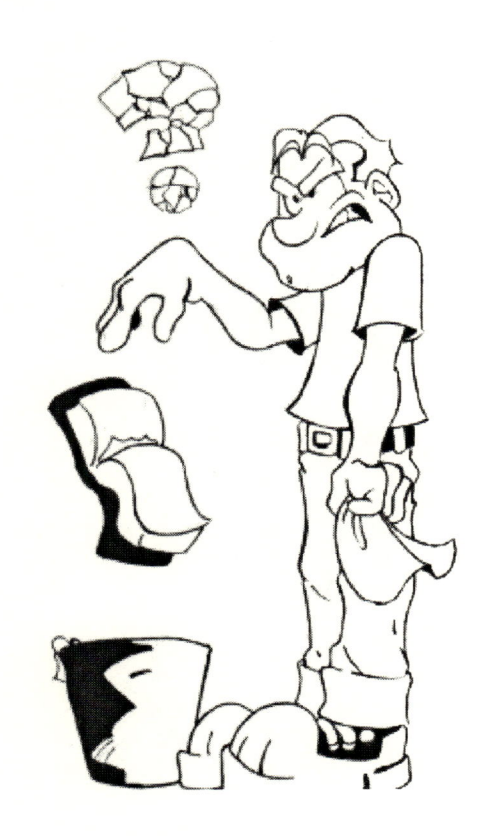

Two bodies have I,
though both joined in one.
The more still I stand,
the quicker I run.

What am I?

A little house full of meat,
but no door to go in and eat.

What am I?

I go up, but at the same time I go down,
Up towards the sky, and down to the ground.

It is present tense and past tense too.
Come for a ride, just me and you.

What am I?

A redhead with a yellow coat.
I come in handy to write a note.

What am I?

What can bring back the dead,
Makes us cry,
Makes us laugh,
Makes us young.

It is born in an instant yet lasts a lifetime.

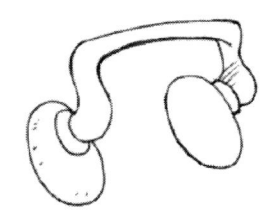

Without a bridle or a saddle,
across a slope I ride a-
straddle.

And those I ride, by help of me,
though almost blind
are made to see.

What am I?

You use it between
your head and toes.
The more it works
the thinner it grows.

What is it?

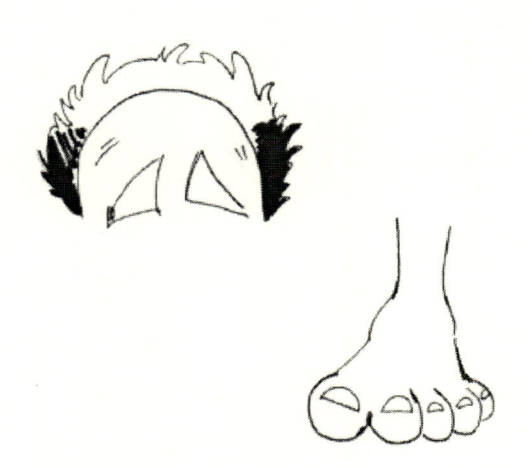

What gets whiter as it gets dirtier?

Everything you catch
you throw away.

But everything you don't
catch, you keep.

What are you hunting?

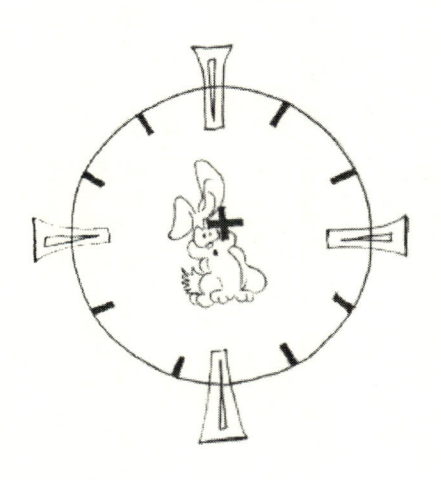

A man looked at a photograph and said, "Brothers and sisters I have none, but that man's father is my father's son."

Who was the person in the photograph?

What has a foot on each side and a foot in the middle?

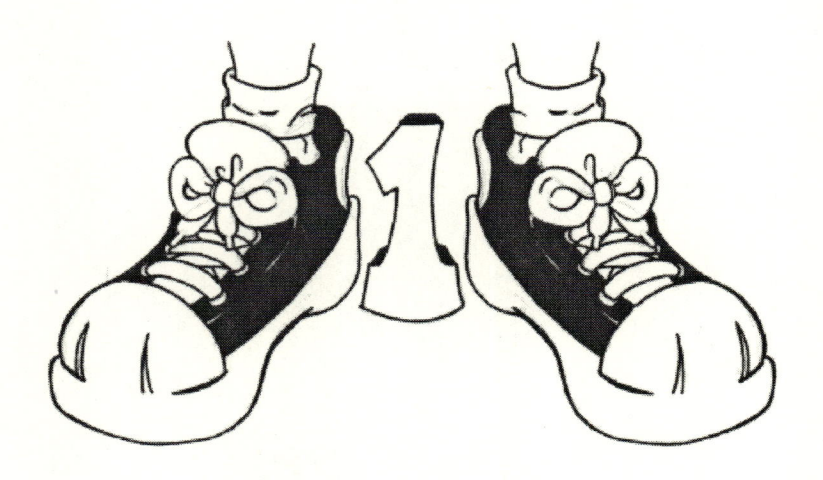

Sometimes I flip,
Other times I just flop.
I tend to stay home when the temperature drops.

But when it starts to get hot,
And the sun comes out,
No need for shoes,
Just wear me out.

What am I?

If you go in the front door, you are at the back.

Where are you?

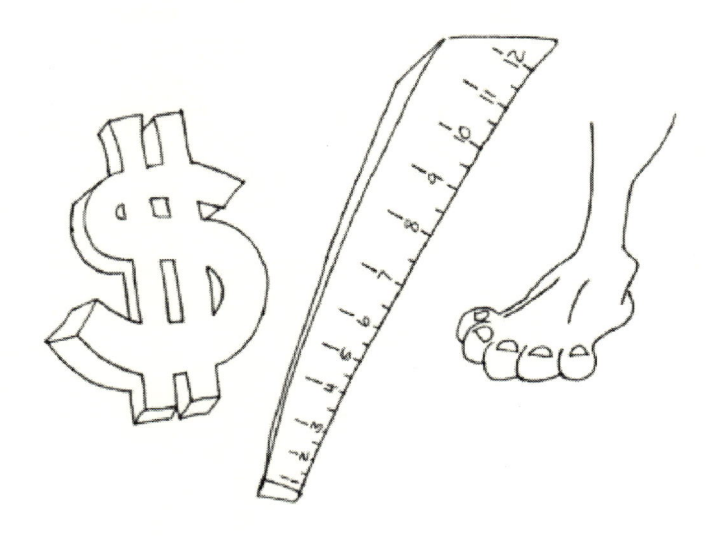

What is bought by the yard and worn by the foot?

Someone else has to take it before you can get it.

What is it?

My voice is tender,
and my waist is slender.

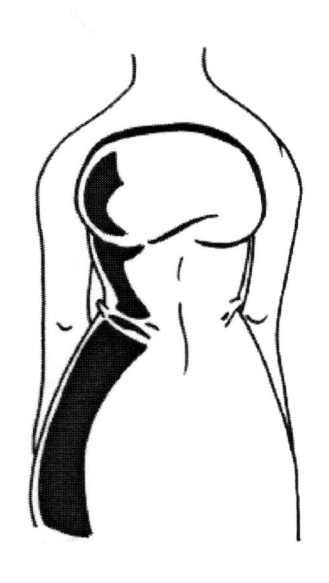

Often invited to play;
Yet, wherever I go
I must take my bow
Or else I have nothing to say.

What am I ?

What makes more noise when it is dead than when it is alive?

I store you children in paper form,
And other materials easily torn.
I am quite small, but can hold lots,
And travel with you, on your buttocks.

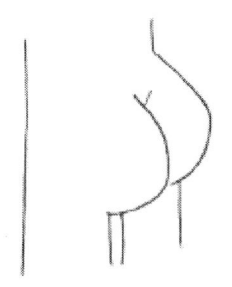

What am I?

I have four main points, but I am round you see. In the bush you would be possibly lost without me.

What am I?

I am amazing because I
have the force,
To hold down a cow or horse.

As you have doubtlessly found,
I am always around,
And I am constantly working
of course!

What am I?

You mix and disrupt me,
but it makes me stronger.

Then you ignore me,
but I get stronger still.

To top it off,
It is surprising to see,
Eventually you end up
walking all over me.

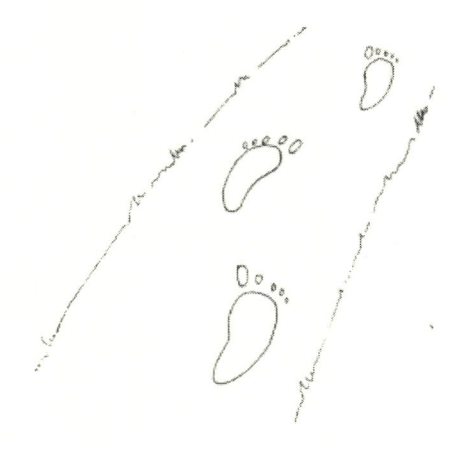

What am I?

Name four days of the week that begin with the letter "T".

First casualties of a small scale war.
Our duty is to defend our lord.
Armed with neither gun nor sword.
One step at a time, we move forward.

What are we?

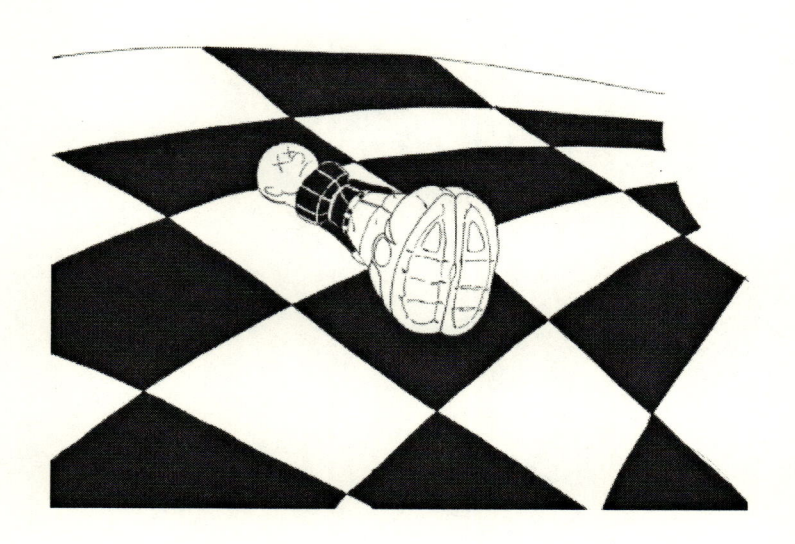

What are two things you cannot get rid of by losing them?

In the grass I am clothed in yellow array.

Near death I turn white, then fly away.

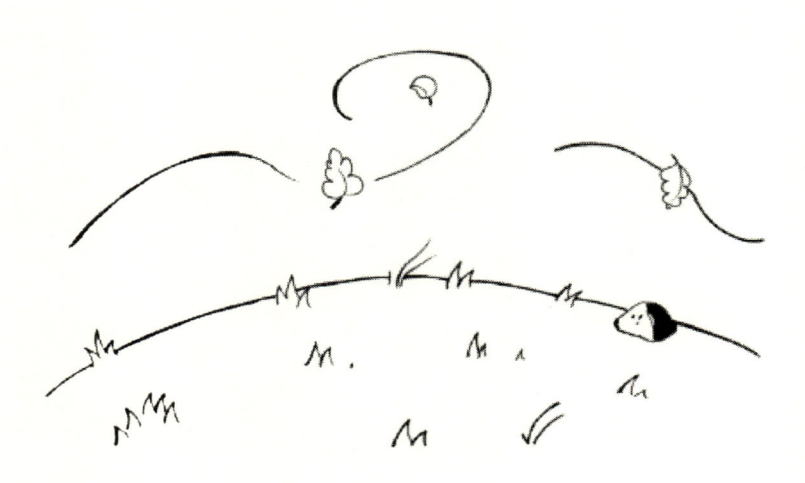

What am I?

I am seen in places that appear to need me not.

I seldom come to places that need me the most.

Sometimes my arrival is celebrated, but other times I am truly hated.

I refresh all things whether they need it or not.

What am I?

What common form of transportation has eight wheels but carries only one passenger?

Dead on the field lie ten soldiers in white,
Struck down by three eyes as black as night.

What's going on here?

Millions through the highway,
Sent all day long.
The post office is lonelier,
Ever since I came along.

What am I?

Sooner or later I will catch you,
Whether coming back or going to.

Sit back, relax, go with the flow.
No need for speed,
You must go slow.

What am I?

Where does love always mean nothing?

They say we are apart,
but we are actually together.

A home you don't own,
to survive the weather.

What are we?

What sits down going up and stands up going down?

I am wanted dead or alive.

Sometimes I am taken,
Sometimes I am not.
My purpose you ask?
To help things get caught.

What am I?

Practice and reflexes is all it takes.
Mistakes can kill you.
Good thing it's all fake.
Fingers and buttons with
two friends or three.
All from the comfort of your own
TV.

What is being described?

If a bottle with its cork costs $1.10, and the bottle costs a dollar more than the cork, how much is the cork?

When I look up its bright,
but when I look down its dark.

What am I?

Once you put some in,
You can never get it out.

Making the most of it,
That's what its all about!

What is it?

Two circles with a common link,
To punish the actions you
should rethink.

And perhaps it was a big mistake;
A key will make my circles break.

What are the circles?

Two sisters are we,
One dark and one fair.
Twin towers shaking,
We're quite the pair.
One from land,
One from sea.

Tell us truly, who are we?

It is my job to poke your snack.
Just grab ahold, then put me back.

But if you'd like, hold me with care,
And clean that something you have
stuck up there.

What am I?

As you sit and shut the door,
you realize its time for more…

More of what you may ask,
but the answer is your task.

But there is no point avoiding
me. I am too close to "E".

What is it?

Be warned!
Your head is in danger.

If bread is at stake,
I will come to a stranger.

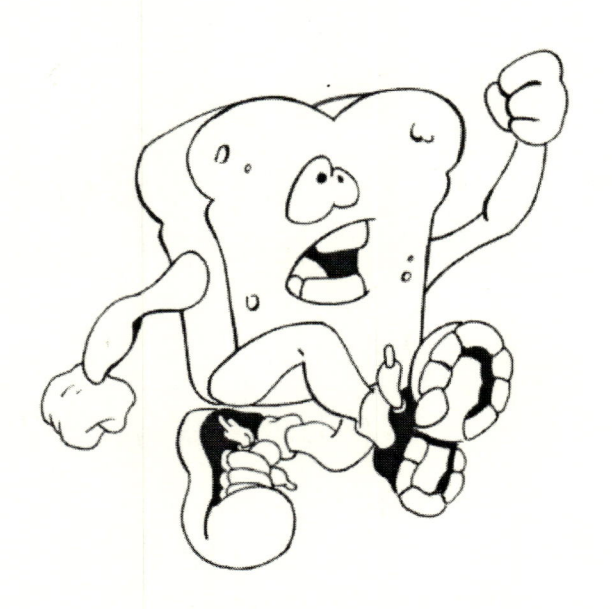

What am I?

Brown-eyed to blue-eyed,
What shall it be?

I will cover your eyes,
But quite clearly you'll see.

At first a bit tricky,
To put on and wear.

To a stranger they're hidden.
Only you know they're there.

What are they?

At one time I connected you to life,
But now closed off forever.

On some I poke out,
On others I stay caved in.

What am I?

Don't bother with tapes.
It is time to update.

I can scratch, but I don't itch.

You can invest in me,
and slowly get rich.

What am I?

What is open when it's closed, and closed when it's open?

One bite at a time;
Always with your help.
Press my jaws together,
A row of teeth lost forever.
But those you can replace.
Handy for the office space.

What am I?

Very attractive,
Yet very repulsive.

You might find me in
the kitchen holding
a job well done.

What am I?

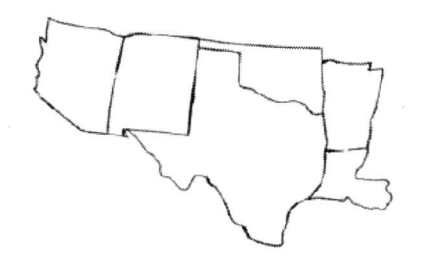

It is obvious what state I'm from,
No need to contemplate.
If you want a good meal,
Do not ever serve this plate.

What am I?

What lays across your waist and chest that can keep your head in one piece?

I will shoot you if you scare me.

Find me in a place where ships are known to sink.

My weapon is loaded with different colored ink.

What am I?

I am music to your ears,
With strings attached my dear.
Although I am always hollow,
Filled with waves I can be.
Sideways I rest,
On top of your knees.

What am I?

There is a man sitting on a chair making loud noises. However, he does not realize he is making them. All of his family is in the same room smiling at each other, knowing its perfectly normal.

What is the man doing?

The floors I roam during morning or night.

In stories of fright, I am known to take flight.

Commonly used to this very day. I push the unwanted up, out and away.

What am I?

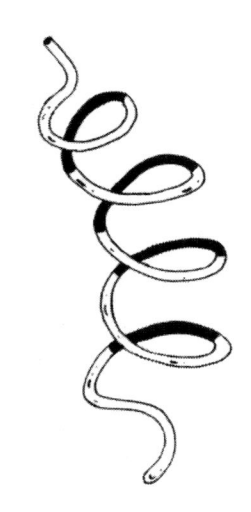

A strip of metal spiraled in,
Capable of holding a hundred
times its size within.

Yet with your fingers and a little
force, you can easily bend it of
course.

What is it?

I went to a field and couldn't get through it, so I went to a school and learned how to do it.

What is it?

The trick is to keep me flat.
I fly much better like that.

Back and forth through the air,
Spinning carefree in flight.

But some dogs do scare me,
They just jump up and bite.

What am I?

Keep your best friend in line at least some of the time.

Only a short distance, and then stiff resistance.

Too long is a joke, but too short might choke.

What is being described?

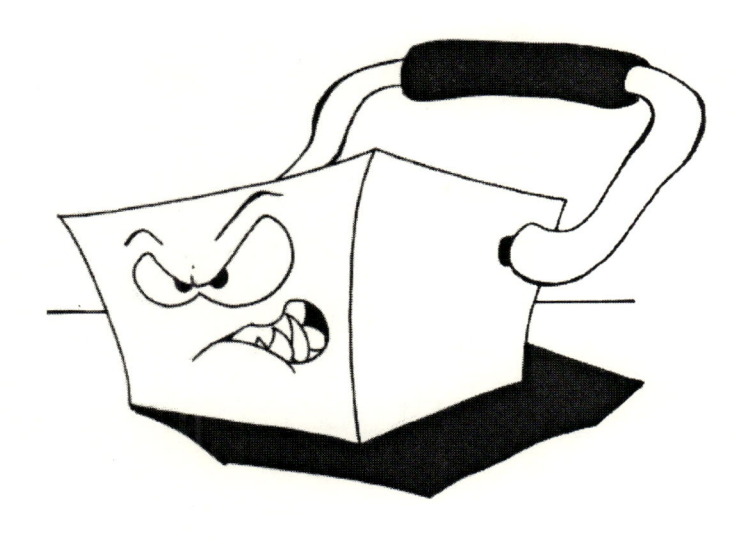

Tips of green I like to eat.
Growling loudly beside the street.

In the summer months,
you will see me more.

Push me around,
It is quite a chore.

What am I?

Take a swing,
You will not see.
Filled with treats
for you and me.

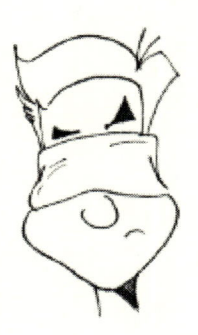

What am I?

You cannot eat me but...

Open up a can,
And serve me fresh.
Bright greenish yellow,
A round ball of mesh.

What am I?

A tube I can be,
But nothing like a pipe.
A crew you might need,
To make things more light.
I will swallow your foot,
But worse I can be,
When I swallow your leg,
Right up to your knee.

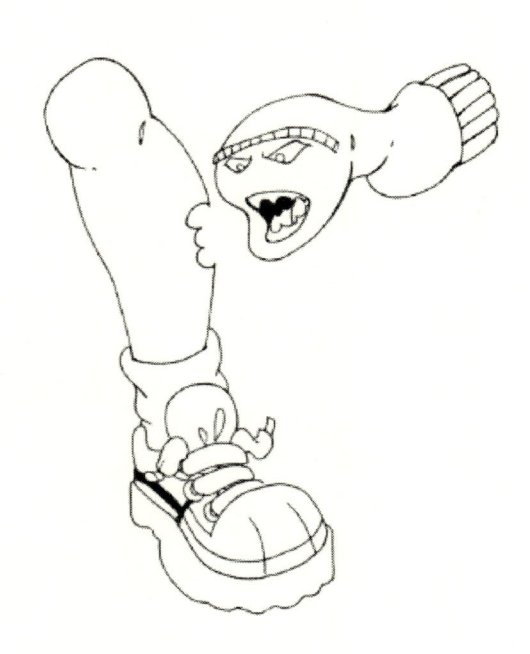

What am I?

When you travel,
You might go through me.

If you are in love,
Your head is in me.

But most importantly,
Just like a theif,
I will take your sunshine,
And cause you grief.

What am I?

A good band will do it.

Soft and light? - I think not

Tell me, what would you get
if you drilled a stone block?

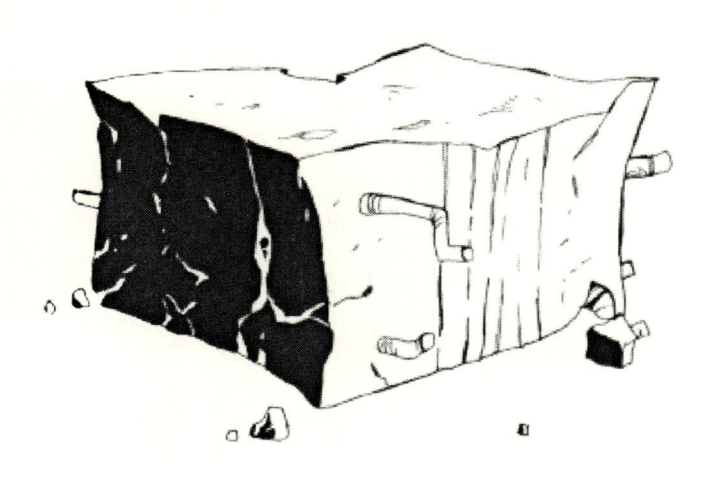

A man builds a house with all four sides facing south.

A bear walks past the house.

What color is the bear?

In a tunnel of darkness lies a beast of iron.

It can only attack when pulled back.

What is it?

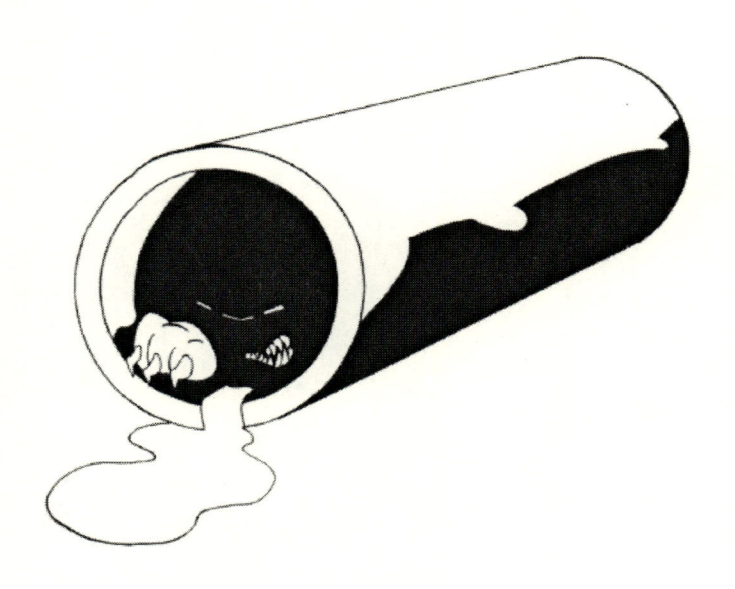

Answers (Odd #s 1- 49)

1. Hug
3. Dominoes
5. Ear of corn. Throw away the husk, cook the ear, and eat the outside,
    and throw away the core.
7. Notes
9. Banana
11. He was playing Monopoly
13. Nothing
15. Silence
17. Charcoal
19. Tug-o-War
21. Moon
23. First, turn on any switch, wait a few minutes, then turn it off.
Next, turn another switch on. Go upstairs. The light that is turned on is obviously the switch that is on. Touch the other two lights. The one that is still hot corresponds to the switch you turned on for a few minutes. The one that is cold corresponds to the switch you never touched.
25. Anchor
27. River
29. The wise man said "Switch camels and race to the city"
31. The car was an automatic.
33. 28 days. The snail doesn't slip when he reaches the top.
35. The dates are in B.C.
37. Mt. Everest - it was still the tallest even though it wasn't discovered yet.
39. Soul
41. 2nd Place
43. Snowman
45. Married people were on the plane. Only "single" people were killed.
47. Golf ball
49. Treadmill

Answers (Even #s 1- 50)

2. DNA
4. Dentist
6. News
8. Beach
10. Coffin
12. Palm Tree
14. Library
16. Wheels
18. Calculator
20. Pillow
22. Batteries
24. Fork (fork in the road, pitch fork)
26. Magnifier
28. Pancakes
30. Lobster
32. Clothes hangers
34. Popcorn kernel
36. Auction
38. Piano
40. Zipper
42. Taking two friends to the movies once is cheaper because otherwise you pay for your own ticket twice.
44. The broken clock. It gives the exact time twice each day.
46. Neither. Crossing paths means they are at the same spot, therefore, they are both the same distance from New York.
48. Autobiography
50. The Great Pyramids

Answers (Odd #s 51-101)

51. An apple a day keeps the doctor away
53. Lawsuit
55. "Thousand"
57. Four. Two of the fathers could be grandfathers, and they are all
    sons.
59. The letter "e"
61. 3 socks. 12 socks.
63. Third. Lions that haven't eaten in 3 years are dead.
65. Onion
67. $1.19 Three quarers, 4 dimes, and 4 pennies.
69. Watermelon
71. Suicide
73. When you are adding time. 11 am plus 2 hours is 1 pm.
75. Zero. If he has 3 labeled correctly, the 4th is labeled correctly too.
77. Windows
79. Priest
81. Last Name
83. Take glass #2 and pour the milk in glass # 5
85. Dictionary
87. Your word
89. Phone/Door Bell
91. Record
93. Courship
95. All of them do
97. Teapot
99. Advice
101. They were a band hired to play at an event.

Answers (Odd #s 52-100)

52. Church
54. Penci Sharpener
56. Jellyfish
58. Vaccum
60. Marathon
62. Your foot
64. Electrical plug
66. Tattoo
68. Fax
70. Wrinkles
72. Peacock
74. Putting on a tie
76. Sugar
78. Umbrella
80. Divorce
82. Camera
84. Lighthouse
86. Insurance
88. Doughnut
90. Arm Pit
92. Castle
94. Sneeze
96. Cheerleaders
98. Three - one rose, one tulip, and one daisy
100. Ants

*A*nswers (Odd #s 103-151)

103. Your breath
105. Footsteps
107. The word "wholesome"
109. Towel/Napkin
111. Secret
113. Name, Mane, Amen, Mean
115. Vote
117. Your lap
119. Splinter
121. A hole
123. Grapes
125. Candle
127. Shoe
129. Darkness/Fog
131. Match
133. Each hour Alicia completes 1/3 of the fence, and Mark completes 1/6 of the fence. So, add these together 1/3(2/6) + 1/6 and you get 1/2. So working together, they would complete 1/2 of the fence each hour. To complete the job, it would take 2 hours.
135. Meat
137. Sunshine
139. Mrs. Smith - 7 Mr. Smith - 5
141. Nine. All daughters have the same brother in common.
143. Tea Bag
145. Dream
147. Water
149. Hourglass
151. See-saw

Answers (Even #s 102-150)

102. Blink
104. Volcano
106. Hurricane
108. Elephant
110. Toast
112. Ice cubes
114. Drum
116. Owl
118. Laughter
120. Mushroom
122. Diamond
124. Internet
126. Ice Cream Truck
128. Fingernails
130. Heart
132. Stoplight
134. Iceburg
136. Nap
138. Lipstick
140. An oyster. It produces a pearl when it has been injured or attacked.
142. Map
144. Eye
146. Bridge
148. "Short"
150. Nut

Answers (Odd #s 153-215)

153. Memories
155. Soap
157. Lice
159. A yardstick
161. Movie Theater
163. A Picture
165. Leaves
167. Compass
169. Concrete
171. Pawns
172. Temper
173. Dandelion
175. Rollerblades
177. Email
179. On the tennis court
181. A Skiier
183. Video games
185. A light swtich
187. Handcuffs
189. Toothpick
191. Duck
193. Belly Button
195. Drawbridge
197. Magnet
199. Seat Belt
201. Guitar
203. Broom
205. Fence
207. Leash
209. Pinata
211. Sock
213. Rock
215. Bullet

Answers (Even #s 152-214)

152. Pencil
154. Glasses
156. Blackboard
158. Son
160. Sandals
162. Carpet
164. Violin
166. Wallet
168. Gravity
170. Tuesday, Thursday, Today, Tomorrow
172. Temper
174. Rain
178. Traffic
180. Apartment
182. Bait
184. $0.05. The bottle costs $1.05
186. Time
188. Salt & Pepper Shaker
190. Gasoline/Fuel
192. Contact Lenses
194. CD
196. Stapler
198. License plate
200. Octopus
202. Snoring
204. Paper Clip
206. Frisbee
208. Lawn Mower
210. Tennis ball
212. Cloud
214. White. It's a polar bear. A house with four sides facing southis at the North Pole.